AMERICAN LEGENDS™

Daniel Boone

Marianne Johnston

The Rosen Publishing Group's
PowerKids Press™
New York

Published in 2001 by The Rosen Publishing Group, Inc.
29 East 21st Street, New York, NY 10010

Copyright © 2001 by The Rosen Publishing Group, Inc.

5/23/02 World media 14.00

First Edition

Book Design: Michael de Guzman

Photo Credits: pp. 4, 11, 12, 15 © North Wind Pictures; p. 7 © Jennie Woodcock; Reflections Photolibrary/CORBIS; p. 8 © CORBIS/Lee Snider; p. 16 © CORBIS; p. 19 © SuperStock; p. 20 Art Resource, Courtesy of The National Portrait Gallery, Smithsonian Institution.

Johnston, Marianne.
       Daniel Boone / Marianne Johnston.
          p. cm.— (American legends)
       Includes index.
       Summary: This book describes the life and the legend of Daniel Boone, who explored the American frontier of the 1700s.
       ISBN 0-8239-5579-6
       1.Boone, Daniel, 1734-1820—Juvenile literature. 2. Pioneers—Kentucky—Biography—Juvenile literature. 3. Kentucky—Biography—Juvenile literature. 4. Frontier and pioneer life—Kentucky—Juvenile literature. [1. Boone, Daniel, 1734-1820. 2. Pioneers. 3. Frontier and pioneer life.] I. Title. II. Series.
       2000
       976.9'02'092—dc21
       [B]

Manufactured in the United States of America

Contents

Daniel Boone was a hunter, trapper, and farmer. He also enjoyed
wandering in the wilderness. Daniel called his dog Cuff. He felt
that having a good dog helped a person succeed in life.

Daniel Boone

A brave **pioneer** named Daniel Boone **roamed** the forests of North America more than 225 years ago. The United States was not even a country then. Daniel Boone was known for his bravery in the **wilderness**. He often explored the wilderness by himself. Wild bears lived in the woods. Daniel could hear the wolves howling at night. He was not afraid, though. In fact the sounds of the forest made Daniel happy, howling wolves and all! The **legendary** Daniel Boone thought fear was a waste of time.

What Is a Legend?

A **legend** is a story that has come down from the past. This type of story is not always about an actual event from the past. Sometimes it goes beyond the truth. This means that a part of the story may have been made up. We make legends out of our heroes. Heroes are people who have **qualities** we admire. Daniel Boone is an example of a hero who has become a legend. Most people would like to be as brave as Daniel Boone. He was a **modest** person who enjoyed the quiet of nature. His good qualities are the center of the stories about him. The stories grow more unreal and charming with each telling. This **exaggeration** makes the stories fun. It also helps us remember the good qualities that Daniel had.

We like to read about legends, or stories that come down to us from earlier times. Parts of these stories might not be true. They can be based on real events or people, but they might include parts that are made up.

Daniel was born in this house on November 2, 1734, in Berks County, Pennsylvania. At that time, Berks County was located on the edge of the Pennsylvania wilderness.

The Ways of the Wilderness

Daniel Boone was born on November 2, 1734, in Berks County, Pennsylvania. At that time, Pennsylvania was still a **colony** of England. Daniel was the 6th of 11 children in the family.

Daniel's childhood home was surrounded by wilderness. Bears, deer, and wolves wandered the forests. Daniel learned his legendary hunting skills there. In those days, a family had to hunt for much of their food. At first Daniel hunted rabbits and squirrels with a small spear. By the time he was 12 years old, he was hunting deer and bear with a rifle. Daniel's hunting provided most of the meat used to feed his family.

Exploration

The Boones left Pennsylvania in 1750. Daniel was 15 years old. The family traveled south on foot. They settled along the Yadkin River in what is today northwestern North Carolina. In North Carolina, Daniel met a young woman named Rebecca Bryan. They got married in 1756. The couple became the parents of 10 children!

Over the years, Daniel explored and hunted. In 1765, he spent six months exploring the wilderness of Florida. Alligators and mosquitoes lived in the swamps he traveled through. Even with these dangers, Daniel still loved outdoor life. He wanted to live in Florida so he could be away from other **settlers**. Rebecca did not like this idea.

Daniel is shown here wearing buckskin. He often hunted male deer, which are called bucks. The hide of one buck sold for about one dollar back in Daniel's day. Today we still use the word "buck" to mean one dollar.

In 1773, Daniel tried to lead a group of settlers through the Cumberland Gap, the area where today's states of Kentucky, Tennessee, and Virginia meet. Native Americans attacked them, and Daniel's oldest son was captured and killed.

Adventures in Kentucky

Daniel thought that where he lived in North Carolina was too crowded. He began to explore the **territory** of Kentucky in 1767. He loved to walk in its thick green woods. It is said that Daniel Boone never got lost in his life. One legend also says he was forced to spend a cold, snowy winter in a cave in the mountains in eastern Kentucky. In 1959, a piece of tree bark with Daniel's name carved on it was found in a cave there.

In 1773, Daniel tried to lead his family and other settlers to Kentucky through the Cumberland Gap, a narrow path through mountains. During the trip, a group of Native Americans attacked them. Daniel and the others had to return home.

The Founding of Boonesborough

Daniel still wanted to settle in Kentucky. In 1775, a trading company hired him and a group of men to blaze a trail through the Cumberland Gap and into Kentucky. To blaze a trail, the men had to mark each tree by cutting off a piece of bark to show where the trail led. The trail was to be used by settlers to start a settlement in Kentucky. This trail became known as the Wilderness Road. It ran from Fort Chiswell, Virginia, to the Ohio River in northern Kentucky. The road was about 250 miles (402 km) long! After they had finished the road, they built a **stockade** along the Kentucky River. They named it Boonesborough. Daniel went back east to bring his family to their new home.

Boonesborough was a very small settlement. The stockade's wooden walls surrounded 26 cabins. The settlers' beds were made from boards covered with animal skins. The nearest place to buy supplies was about 200 miles (300 km) away.

This is one artist's idea of how Daniel overtook the Shawnee when he rescued his daughter and her friends in 1778. Most likely, though, there would have been more struggling and disorder during the rescue.

Fights With Native Americans

Life in Boonesborough was dangerous. The settlers fought the Native Americans in the area. One group of Native Americans, the **Shawnee**, was especially angry. Settlers such as the Boones were moving into the Shawnee's territory and taking the land. The Shawnee feared they would not have any land left for their own families. They fought very hard to keep the land. Sometimes the Shawnee attacked the stockade. The settlers had to be careful when they went outside Boonesborough. One day, one of Daniel's daughters and two of her friends were in a canoe on the river. The Shawnee **kidnapped** the girls. After three days of tracking them, Daniel and some other men rescued the girls.

Captured by the Shawnee

In 1778, the Shawnee kidnapped Daniel, too. He was taken to the camp of Blackfish, the leader of the Shawnee. Blackfish decided not to kill Daniel. Instead he adopted Daniel as his son. The Shawnee scrubbed Daniel down in the icy waters of the river to "take his white blood out." It was February, so it was probably very cold! They cut off his hair except for a small lock on the top of his head. After about four months of living with the Shawnee, Daniel escaped. When he got back to Boonesborough, he found that his family had returned to North Carolina. Rebecca thought that Daniel had been killed. Daniel and his wife soon found each other again.

Artist H. Charles McBarron shows the legendary Daniel Boone overpowering the Shawnee on January 6, 1778. In fact, though, Daniel and 25 other men were captured by the Shawnee while they were exploring for salt deposits.

In 1800, Daniel was named a magistrate, or judge, of the area where he and Rebecca lived. He was called on by the people to settle disagreements and rule on fights about property. His decisions were respected by everyone.

Daniel's Last Adventure

For the next 20 years, the Boones moved around in Kentucky and Virginia. Daniel thought it was getting too crowded in these areas. In 1799, Daniel had his last adventure on the **frontier**. He was almost 65 years old when he and his family set out for Missouri. Few settlers had moved to the territory of Missouri. This huge area was located west of the Mississippi River. Legend says Daniel and his daughter's husband made the long journey to Missouri from Kentucky entirely on foot. The rest of his family traveled by canoe.

The Boones stayed in Missouri until they died. Rebecca died at age 73 in 1813. Daniel died seven years later at the age of 85.

Remembering Daniel Boone

Many towns, parks, and schools in Kentucky, North Carolina, Virginia, and Tennessee are named for Daniel Boone.

In the 1820s, a writer named James Fenimore Cooper wrote a series of books about a brave frontiersman, Natty Bumppo, also called Leatherstocking. It is said that the figure of Leatherstocking is based on Daniel Boone.

Today you can visit the site of Boonesborough, Kentucky. It has been rebuilt to look the way it did in the days when Daniel roamed the frontier. Actors wear the clothing of that time period. You can also visit frontier cabins. They are furnished just as they would have been when the Boones lived there.

Glossary

colony (KAH-luhn-ee) An area in a new territory where a large group of people move, who are still ruled by the leaders and laws of their old country.

exaggeration (ihg-zah-juh-RAY-shun) Something made to seem larger or more amazing than it really is.

frontier (frun-TEER) The edge of a settled country, where the wilderness begins.

kidnapped (KID-napt) To have stolen or carried off a person by force.

legend (LEH-jend) A story passed down through the years that many people believe.

legendary (LEH-jen-der-ee) To be famous and important.

modest (MOD-ist) Not thinking too highly of oneself.

pioneer (py-uh-NEER) One of the first people to settle in a new area.

qualities (KWAH-luh-teez) Features that make something or someone special.

roamed (ROHMD) To have walked around with no special plan.

settlers (SEH-tuh-lers) People who move to a new land to live.

Shawnee (shah-NEE) Native Americans who lived in the Ohio valley, which includes Kentucky.

stockade (stah-KAYD) A wooden wall made of large, strong posts. The posts are put upright in the ground to help protect the area inside the wall.

territory (TEHR-uh-tohr-ee) Land that is controlled by a person or a group of people.

wilderness (WIL-dur-nis) An area that is wild and has no permanent settlements.

Index

Web Sites

To learn more about Daniel Boone, check out these Web sites:
http://www.berksweb.com/boone.html
http://www.state.ky.us/agencies/parks/ftboones.htm